AND THE BULLFROGS SING

A LIFE CYCLE BEGINS

by DAVID L. HARRISON

illustrated by KATE COSGROVE

HOLIDAY HOUSE • NEW YORK

IT is spring. Time to find a mate. A male bullfrog sings loud and deep, *rumm rumm rumm*.

A female bullfrog likes his song. Before long she lays eggs.

She lays them in sheets on the surface of the pond.

A fish tries to eat an egg. Yuck! To some fish, bullfrog eggs taste bad. The eggs hatch. The babies have no legs. They have tails. They can only breathe underwater. They are not frogs yet. They are tadpoles.

The tadpoles nibble plants. They nibble algae.
They grow fatter and begin to grow legs.

Their tails grow shorter. They can breathe air.
Now they are little bullfrogs.

Little bullfrogs taste good.
Yum! Fish love to eat them.
So do turtles, birds, snakes,
and big bullfrogs.

Bullfrogs don't chew their food. They gulp
it down—wings, fins, bones, and all.

The little bullfrogs like to eat. All they do is eat and hide. If a fly buzzes by, a long tongue shoots out—

Zap! Bye-bye, fly.

If a spider crawls by—
Zap! Bye-bye, spider.

If a tiny fish swims by—
Splash! Gulp! Bye-bye, fish.

The little bullfrogs eat and grow all summer. They grow all fall. They are not little anymore. They are midsize.

Winter comes. Nights grow cold.
Frogs are cold-blooded. They need
sunshine to keep warm.

Big frogs jump into the pond.
Midsize frogs jump in too.

On the muddy bottom, their hearts slow down. They breathe through their skin. They look like they are asleep. They are hibernating.

Spring comes. The bullfrogs wake up hungry.
They hop out of the pond. The midsize
bullfrogs eat fat worms, moths, little lizards,
even little frogs!

It is time to find a mate. The big male bullfrogs sing on the bank for female bullfrogs, *rumm rumm rumm*.

The midsize bullfrogs sing too. Their voices are midsize, *rumm rumm rumm*. The females choose the older, bigger males.

The midsize bullfrogs eat
and grow all spring.

They grow all summer.

Fall comes. They have grown into big bullfrogs.

Winter comes. The bullfrogs
hibernate on the bottom of the pond.

Spring comes. Time to find mates. Birds whistle for mates. Crickets chirp for mates. Foxes yip for mates.

And the bullfrogs sing, *rumm rumm rumm*. A female picks her favorite singer. Soon there will be more tadpoles.

MORE ABOUT BULLFROGS

Bullfrogs are

- the biggest frogs in North America

Bullfrogs can

- weigh one and one half pounds
- leap more than four feet
- live up to ten years
- stay underwater all winter
- take in oxygen through their skin

Female bullfrogs

- don't croak as often as males
- are bigger than males

Bullfrogs have teeth, but they are very small.

Bullfrog tongues attach in the front of their mouths.

OTHER CHILDREN'S BOOKS ABOUT FROGS

Frogs, by Elizabeth Carney. National Geographic Children's Books, 2009

From Tadpole to Frog, by Kathleen Weidner Zoehfeld. Scholastic Reader Level 1. Scholastic Paperbacks, 2011

SELECTED ONLINE REFERENCES

Wildlife Journal Junior
http://www.nhptv.org/wild/bullfrog.asp

Defenders of Wildlife
http://www.defenders.org/frogs/basic-facts

Nature Mapping Program
http://naturemappingfoundation.org/natmap/facts/american_bullfrog_712.html

Bullfrogs
http://www.bullfrogs.com/Bullfrog-Life-Cycle.html

To Robin and Jeff with love.
No dad could wish for more!
—D. L. H
For Juniper, who would never ever *ever* eat a fly.
—K. C.

The publisher thanks José Rosado of The Harvard Museum of Comparative Biology
and Lauren Vonnahme, B.S., Biology, for their expert review of the text.

Text copyright © 2019 by David L. Harrison • Illustrations copyright © 2019 by Kate Cosgrove
All Rights Reserved • HOLIDAY HOUSE is registered in the U.S. Patent and Trademark Office.
Printed and bound in November 2018 at Tien Wah Press, Johor Bahru, Johor, Malaysia.
The artwork was created with pencils and digital tools. • www.holidayhouse.com • First Edition
1 3 5 7 9 10 8 6 4 2
Library of Congress Cataloging-in-Publication Data

Names: Harrison, David L. (David Lee), 1937– author. | Cosgrove, Kate, illustrator.
Title: And the bullfrogs sing: a life cycle begins / by David L. Harrison ; illustrated by Kate Cosgrove.
Description: First edition. | New York, NY : Holiday House, [2019] | Audience: Ages 4–8.
Audience: K to grade 3. Identifiers: LCCN 2017055732 | ISBN 9780823438341 (hardcover)
Subjects: LCSH: Bullfrog—Life cycles—Juvenile literature. | Frogs—Juvenile literature.
Classification: LCC QL668.E27 H365 2019 | DDC 597.8/92—dc23
LC record available at https://lccn.loc.gov/2017055732